D0884687

MAR 1 5

BALL GAME MATH

KATIE MARSICO

Lerner Publications Company • Minneapolis

For my husband, Carl Marsico

Lerner Publications Company
A division of Lerner Publishing Group, Inc.
241 First Avenue North
Minneapolis, MN 55401 USA

For reading levels and more information, look up this title at www.lernerbooks.com.

Photo Acknowledgments
The images in this book are used with the permission of: © iStockphoto.com/Willard, p. 1; © Jupiterimages/Stockbyte/ Thinkstock, p. 4; © brentmelissa/iStock/Thinkstock, p. 5; © Chris Clinton/The Image Bank/Getty Images, p. 6; © MihaelDechev/ Collection/Thinkstock, p. 7 (volleyball); © iStockphoto.com/spxChrome, pp. 7, 9, 11, 13, 17, 19, 23, 25, 27 (spiral notebook); © iStockphoto.com/CEFutcher, p. 8; © iStockphoto.com/stuartbur, p. 9 (goggles); © iStockphoto.com/alubalish, pp. 9, 13, 17, 25. 37 (torn paper); © Catalin Petolea/Shutterstock.com, p. 10; © iStockphoto.com/Andyd, p. 11, © iStockphoto. com/squaredpixels, p. 12; © sunstock/iStock/Thinkstock, p. 13 (calendar); © iStockphoto.com/francisblack, p. 14; © Jupiterimages/Photos.com/Thinkstock, p. 15; © blue jean images/Getty Images, p. 16; © iStockphoto.com/cglade, p. 17 (sundae); © iStockphoto.com/RichVintage, p. 18; © iStockphoto.com/gpflman, p. 19 (scoreboard); © Fuse/Thinkstock, p. 20; © iStockphoto.com/Viorika, p. 21; © iStockphoto.com/bmcent1, p. 22; © iStockphoto.com/skynesher, p. 23 (gymnast); © Amy Myers/iStock/Thinkstock, p. 24; © Mark Cunningham/Getty Images, p. 25 (Cabrera); © Jupiterimages/Stockbyte/Thinkstock, p. 26; © iStockphoto.com/kmisphotos, p. 27 (lacrosse stick); © Todd Strand/Independent Picture Service, p. 28; © photokup/ Shutterstock.com, p. 29.

Front Cover: © Dave and Les Jacobs/Blend Images/Thinkstock, (baseball glove); © iStockphoto.com/rusm, (graph paper).
Back Cover: © iStockphoto.com/zlisjak.

Main body text set in Conduit ITC Std 14/18. Typeface provided by International Typeface Corp.

Library of Congress Cataloging-in-Publication Data

Marsico, Katie, 1980–
    Ball game math / by Katie Marsico.
      pages   cm — (Math everywhere!)
    Includes index.
    ISBN 978–1–4677–1885–1 (lib. bdg. : alk. paper)
    ISBN 978–1–4677–4694–6 (eBook)
     1. Mathematics—Juvenile literature. 2. Sports—Mathematics—Juvenile literature.
  3. Word problems (Mathematics)—Juvenile literature. I. Title.
  GV1060.55.M27 2015
  513—dc23   2013041745

Manufactured in the United States of America
1 – CG – 7/15/14

TABLE OF CONTENTS

DISTANCE AROUND THE DIAMOND

Batter up! Sports are exciting. So is math! And without math, sports would not exist. Need proof? Step onto the softball field!

Actually, Sara wishes she could do just that. She and her friends had planned to play softball at the park today. But her brother Sal and his pals already have a game going on the field. Should Sara pack up and head home?

Sal says no. He tells Sara she can make her own field. The meadow alongside the playground would be the perfect spot! Sara hates to admit it, but sometimes big brothers have good ideas.

There's only one little problem. The meadow is about three-fourths of the size of a regular softball field. Sara and Sal know that a softball field usually has a perimeter of 240 feet (73 meters).

A softball field's perimeter = the sum of the lengths of its sides.

The field is shaped like a diamond. So its four sides are always of equal length. There's a base on each of the diamond's four corners.

Sal offers to help Sara get started. He calls a time-out from his game to run to the field house for a tape measure. Next, he helps Sara set up her field in the meadow.

How far apart should they space her bases?

DO THE MATH!

Pretend you're playing with Sara and her friends. You're pitching first. You know how to throw a mean curveball! What you don't know is where to stand. Normally, the pitcher's mound is 40 feet (12 m) from home plate. But remember that this field is one-fourth smaller than usual. How far from home plate should you pitch today?

Check your answers to all questions on pages 30–31.

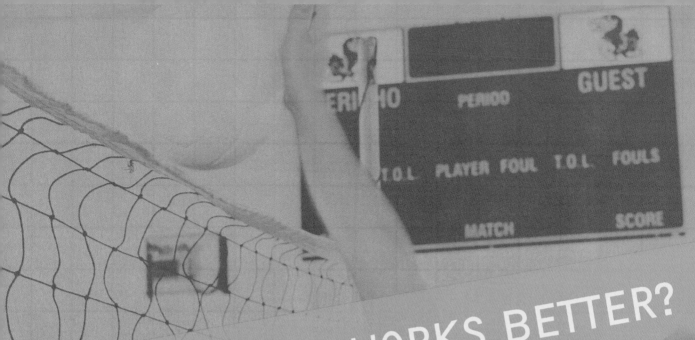

WHICH BALL WORKS BETTER?

Not again! CJ's volleyball hits the net for the fifth time today. He's struggling with his serve. His ball isn't clearing the net.

Coach Jill shakes her head. Something doesn't make sense. Suddenly, she has an idea. She heads to the ball cart. Coach Jill brings back a new volleyball. She suspects it just might do the trick.

She's right! Soon, CJ is serving like a pro again. What was different about the volleyballs? Coach Jill says it was their sizes. The second ball was bigger. That made it easier for CJ to control.

CJ plans to buy his own volleyball. He wants extra practice at home. Coach Jill tells him to pay attention to circumference as he shops. Circumference is the distance around the edge of a circle.

She explains that a ball's circumference = 3.14 × its diameter.
The diameter is the distance through the middle of the ball, from one side to the other.

Coach Jill says CJ's new ball should have a circumference of *at least* 31 inches (79 centimeters).

Later, CJ visits the sporting goods store. He looks at several volleyballs. The one he likes best has a diameter of 8.3 inches (21 cm).

Is it the right size for CJ?

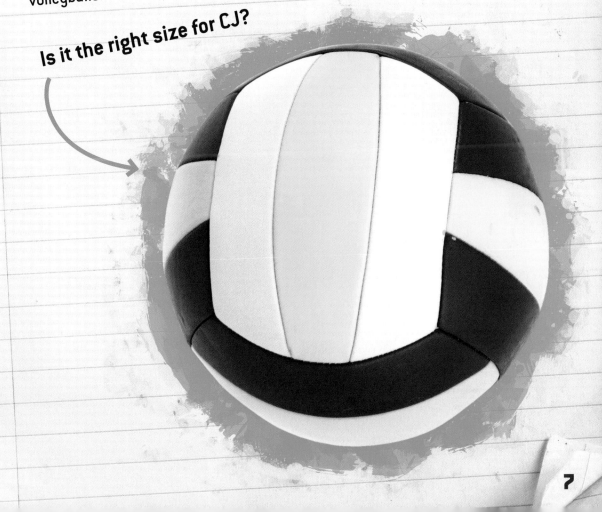

THE LENGTH OF A LAP

Eme adjusts her swim cap. She's captain of her school's swim team. There's a big meet tomorrow.

Eme isn't nervous, though. She knows that practice makes perfect. That's why she swims laps four times a week.

The distance of one lap = the length of the pool.

The school pool is 25 meters (82 ft.) long.

Eme is almost ready to go home. It's 5:15 p.m. She needs to eat dinner and rest up. But first, she must prepare for tomorrow's 100-meter (328 ft.) freestyle event.

Eme decides to practice swimming 100 meters. She plans to do this three times. Then she can dry off and head home.

How many laps must Eme do to swim 100 meters? How many meters will she swim before she leaves?

DO THE MATH!

Splash! Imagine you're in swim class. You use the same pool Eme does. But your teacher always talks about swimming in yards instead of meters. In today's class, he tells you to swim the backstroke for 75 yards (69 m). Then he asks you to practice the breaststroke for 50 yards (46 m). Keep in mind that 1 yard (0.9 m) = 3 feet. How many laps will you swim altogether?

TAKE TWO!

It's so quiet on the tennis court that Mark and Paul could hear a pin drop. The only noise is the soft *thunk* of their rackets hitting the ball. The boys are playing an intense match. It's their second set. A tennis match has two or three sets. Either Mark or Paul must win two of them to become champion.

Sets 1 and 2 are made up of games. For kids Mark and Paul's age, the first player to get four points wins a game. The first person to win four games wins a set. If a player wins set 1 *and* set 2, he wins the match! If each player wins one of the first two sets, the players play a third set. The winner of that set is whoever scores seven points first.

Sound a little tricky? Tennis can be. Luckily, Mark and Paul understand the rules. They're also pretty good at math.

There were five games in set 1. Mark won the first (4–2), second (4–3), fourth (4–1), and fifth (4–3). Paul won the third (4–2).

So far, there have been six games in set 2. Paul won the first (4–1), third (4–2), and fourth (4–2). Mark won the second (4–2), fifth (4–3), and sixth (4-1). The boys have just started game 7. Paul has two points. Mark has one.

How many more points must Mark score to win the entire match? How about Paul?

ON THE FIELD FULL-TIME

Beth can't get her mind off soccer! It is her favorite sport. But she also likes golf, volleyball, and swimming. And sports are only part of the big picture. Beth has school and homework too. So she needs to find out just how much time soccer will take this year. Then she can decide whether she has time for any other sports.

Beth and her mom study Beth's schedule. First, they look at their calendar. Then they reread a letter from the coach. The letter mentions that there are two soccer seasons per school year. One is in the fall. The other is in the spring.

Each soccer season lasts eight weeks. There's a game every Saturday. Practice is on Tuesdays and Thursdays. And there's a four-day training camp in the summer.

Beth knows she'd enjoy being on the team. The question is whether she has enough time to participate. **If Beth signs up for the team, how many days would she end up playing soccer this year?**

DO THE MATH!

Let's say you've joined a soccer league. Today is the first practice. The coach says to show up at 4:30 p.m. Practice lasts 1 hour and 15 minutes. Your dad drops you off. You hug him and head for the field. Wait a second! Did you forget to tell him something? What time should he come back?

HOW MANY FACE-OFFS?

What does Ty love more than zipping across the ice with his hockey stick? Not much! Perhaps the only thing he enjoys more is facing off against his cousin Pete.

A new hockey season is about to begin. It marks the second year the boys have played on opposing teams. They're both members of the same league.

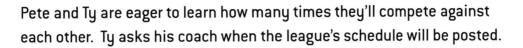

Pete and Ty are eager to learn how many times they'll compete against each other. Ty asks his coach when the league's schedule will be posted.

Coach Ben says he's not sure. Yet he still offers to help Ty answer his question. Coach Ben explains that six teams make up the league. They each have one game every Saturday during the 10-week spring season.

Two teams will play from 5:30 p.m. to 6:10 p.m. Another pair will hit the ice from 6:10 p.m. to 6:50 p.m. The final group will compete from 6:50 p.m. to 7:30 p.m. Pete's team will go up against each of the five other league teams an equal number of times.

How often will Ty's team take on Pete's team in the rink?

FAST FRIENDS

Ready, set, race! Lin and Amy are best friends. They're also good sports. The girls compete against each other in track. Lin beats Amy at some meets. Amy places ahead of Lin at others.

This morning, they will run an 800-meter (875 yd.) event. Lin sped past Amy in the same race last Saturday. They were six seconds apart. Lin won first place. Amy came in third. She finished in 2 minutes, 44 seconds.

Today, the girls make a deal. Lin offers to treat Amy to ice cream after the meet. But there's a hitch. Amy must beat Lin's time from last week. And she has to beat it by at least five seconds! Otherwise, Amy will pay at the ice cream parlor. Amy loves ice cream. And she likes hanging out with Lin. So she agrees.

Both track stars give it their all. Amy is seven seconds faster than she was last week. Meanwhile, Lin shaves two seconds off her own time.

What was Lin's time last week? What are the girls' times this week? Who will end up with a free sundae?

DO THE MATH!

How fast can you move your feet? Pretend you do a 400-meter (437 yd.) dash. You finish in 1 minute, 12 seconds. What is your speed? Speed = distance ÷ time. Remember, 1 minute = 60 seconds.

HOW MANY PLAYS PER PLAYER?

Touchdown! Shane leaps off the bench in excitement. His football team just scored again! They're well on their way to triumph!

Can Shane bring them even closer to victory? He hopes so. It's only the second quarter. Shane's already been part of several impressive plays. His league's football games are divided into four quarters of 10 minutes each. Each quarter is made up of 24 plays. At any given moment, 11 players per team are in the game.

Shane and his 21 teammates never feel shortchanged when it comes to time on the field. That's because Coach Brad is always fair. Everyone on the team participates in an equal number of plays per game.

In this game, Shane had 11 plays in the first quarter. So far, he's also had three in the second.

How many more times should Shane expect to head onto the field before the game ends?

PLAY BETTER, SCORE BIGGER!

Jim plans to command the basketball court this season. He has learned a lot about the game. But Jim wants to keep improving. His goal for the season is to score more points than he did last year.

Jim sits down with Coach Mike. Jim asks the coach how many points he scored last year. Coach Mike scratches his head. There's a little problem. He left his scorebook at home.

Wait a second! Coach Mike searches his office. He still has his old playbook. It doesn't list overall scores for each player. But it *does* note what shots they made during last season's games.

Jim played nine games last year. Coach Mike says he scored six free throws. He also made eight field goals. Of those, five were within the three-point line. And three were outside the three-point line.

Jim knows that a free throw = 1 point.
Field goals made within the three-point line = 2 points.
Field goals made outside the three-point line = 3 points.

How many points did Jim score last season?

NO AVERAGE ATHLETE

Anne is awesome at uneven bars. She always wows the gymnastics judges. Coach Sue is also impressed. She tells Anne that she flips and swings between two raised bars like a circus trapeze artist.

Coach Sue is thinking about putting Anne on the gold team. Right now, Anne's on the silver team. Members of the gold team get to compete in more meets and attend special training camps. Anne wants to go for the gold!

So far, she's participated in five meets. Anne is always one of her team's top scorers. Yet she's never gotten a 10. That's the highest score the judges can give. She's come close, though!

Anne scored 9.0 at her first meet. Then she got 9.2 at two meets in a row. At her last two meets, her scores were 9.1 and 9.3.

Coach Sue tells Anne she's proud of her. She's almost ready to add her to the gold team. The coach just wants to watch her at one more meet. She'd like Anne to boost her average score up to 9.2.

Her average score = the sum of her scores ÷ the sum of her meets.

Anne does her absolute best at the sixth meet. And it shows. The judges give her a 9.4! Anne is thrilled. **But is it enough to earn a spot on the gold team?**

SHOW OFF THOSE STATS!

Martin plays Little League baseball. Yet he has far bigger plans for his future. Martin dreams of being a professional baseball player. Maybe he'll even get to bat on the same field as Miguel Cabrera! Cabrera is Martin's hero and a Major League Baseball (MLB) star. He plays first base for the Detroit Tigers. Martin knows almost everything about Cabrera. This includes his MLB statistics, or stats. A stat is a number that represents a piece of information.

So what's Cabrera's most impressive stat? He had the highest MLB batting average in 2013. **Batting average = a player's base hits ÷ how many times he's been at bat.** Cabrera's batting average that year was .348. So he made base hits almost 35 percent of the time he went to bat.

Will Martin outplay Cabrera one day? He believes he has what it takes. In fact, Martin suspects he already has a better batting average! Of course, Martin doesn't face MLB pitchers.

Martin played 10 games last season. He was up to bat 23 times. He had 14 base hits. **What was Martin's batting average? How much higher was his batting average than Cabrera's in 2013?**

DO THE MATH!

What's your strikeout rate? Let's say you pitched 20 innings over the past two seasons. You struck a batter out eight times. There are usually six innings in a Little League game. How many batters do you strike out for every six innings you pitch? Strikeouts per 6 innings pitched = (the number of times you've struck a batter out ÷ the number of innings you've pitched) × 6.

CAMP COMPETITION

Helen, Leah, and Claire are crazy about lacrosse! It's a blend of their favorite sports. Lacrosse involves skills they use in basketball, soccer, and hockey.

The girls are their team's strongest players. They're also good friends. So they'll be happy no matter who wins a spot at lacrosse camp. The camp is for the best players in the state. Coach Pat tells Helen, Leah, and Claire that they're all talented players. But she can send only one of them to camp. How will the coach decide who should go?

First, Coach Pat will look at their scoring averages.
A player's scoring average = the number of goals she's scored ÷ the number of games she's played.

Next, the coach will review their save percentages. Each girl played goalie for one game this season.
A player's save percentage = the number of saves she's made ÷ (the number of saves she's made + the number of goals she's allowed).

Coach Pat will then add each player's scoring average and save percentage together. Whoever ends up with the highest number will go to camp!

Helen, Leah, and Claire played eight games this season. Helen scored 13 goals. She made nine saves and allowed three goals. Leah scored 15 goals. She made seven saves and allowed four goals. Claire scored 14 goals. She made eight saves and allowed four goals. **Which girl will end up at lacrosse camp?**

DO THE MATH!

Feel like a little lacrosse? Imagine trying out for a youth league. The coaches have to pick two teams. Each team has 12 spots. Be sure to shine on the field! You're up against 35 other hopeful athletes. What percentage of you will make the cut?

READY, SET, KICK!

Do you feel like heading to the nearest batting cage, tennis court, or ice rink? Well, you can start doing your favorite sports activities in a minute. First, though, get ready to solve a few final problems. It won't take long. Then hit the field, court, pool, or rink!

Grab your uniform and ball! Today kicks off the fall soccer season. This year, you'll be playing in a third-grade league. Your coach tells you to prepare for some changes.

For one thing, you'll be using a much bigger field. Last year, your field measured 20 yards (18 m) by 30 yards (27 m). The area of the third-grade field is four times as large. **A soccer field's area is measured in square yards = length × width.** Fortunately, the defensive players have to play on only half of it.

How much extra area will you have to cover on defense this season?

Another difference from last year is game time. Second graders play four quarters of 10 minutes each. Your coach says third-grade games are made up of two halves of 30 minutes each.

How many extra minutes will you spend on the soccer field every Saturday?

Finally, this year's going to be different because you plan to play harder and win bigger than ever before! The coach says last year his top players scored an average of two to three goals per game. You plan to prove that you belong at the top too. Second- and third-grade teams play 16 games a year. Last year, you scored a total of 11 goals.

How many more will you need to make this year to match the coach's all-time best players?

Answer Key

Page 5   Sara and Sal should space the bases 45 feet (14 m) apart. (240 ft. × ¾ the size of a regular field = 180 ft.; 180 ft. ÷ 4 sides = 45 ft. per side)

Do the Math!
You should pitch 30 feet (9 m) from home plate today. (40 ft. × ¾ the size of a regular field = 30 ft.)

Page 7   No. CJ needs a ball that measures *at least* 31 inches (76 cm). This ball has a circumference of 26 inches (66 cm). (3.14 × 8.3 in. = 26 in.)

Page 9   Eme must do four laps to swim 100 meters (330 ft.). (100 m ÷ 25 m per lap = 4 laps)
She will swim 300 meters (984 ft.) before she leaves. (100 m × 3 times = 300 m)

Do the Math!
You will swim five laps altogether. (75 yds. + 50 yds. = 125 yds.; 125 yds. × 3 ft. per yd. = 375 ft.; 375 ft. ÷ 82 ft. = 4.6 laps, or about 5 laps)

Page 11   Mark needs three more points to win the entire match. (He'll win two sets—and the entire match—if he wins game 7; 4 points needed to win game 7 – 1 point he has already scored = 3 points needed to win the entire match.)
Paul needs nine more points to win the entire match. (He'll win one set if he wins game 7, but he'll still need to win set 3 to win the entire match; 4 points needed to win game 7 – 2 points he has already scored = 2 points; 2 points needed to win game 7 + 7 points needed to win set 3 = 9 points needed to win the entire match.)

Page 13   Beth would play soccer 52 days this year. (8 weeks × 2 seasons = 16 total weeks; 1 game + 2 practices = 3 times playing per week; 16 weeks × 3 days per week = 48 days of playing; 48 days of season play + 4 days of camp = 52 total days)

Do the Math!
Your dad should come back at 5:45 p.m. (4:30 p.m. + 1:15 = 5:45 p.m.)

Page 15   Ty's team will take on Pete's team two times. (10 weeks × 1 game per week = 10 games; 10 games ÷ 5 opposing teams = 2 times that the same teams will play each other)

Page 17   Lin's time last week was 2 minutes, 38 seconds. (2:44 – 0:06 = 2:38)
Amy's time this week is 2 minutes, 37 seconds. (2:44 – 0:07 = 2:37)
Lin's time this week is 2 minutes, 36 seconds. (2:38 – 0:02 = 2:36)
Lin will end up with a free sundae. (Amy *did* beat Lin's time last week, but only by 1 second, not 5 seconds; 2:38 – 2:37 = 0:01)

Do the Math!
Your speed is 5.6 seconds per meter. (60 sec. + 12 sec. = 72 sec.; 400 m ÷ 72 sec. = 5.6 sec. per m)

Page 19   Shane should expect to head onto the field 34 more times before the game ends. (22 total players ÷ 11 players at a time = 2; 24 plays per quarter × 4 quarters = 96 total plays per game; 96 total plays ÷ 2 = 48 plays; 11 plays + 3 plays = 14 plays already played; 48 total plays – 14 plays already played = 34 plays left)

Page 21 Jim scored 25 points last season. (6 free throws × 1 point = 6 points; 5 field goals × 2 points = 10 points; 3 field goals × 3 points = 9 points; 6 points + 10 points + 9 points = 25 points)

Page 23 Yes, Anne's new average score is enough to earn a spot on the gold team. (9.0 + 9.2 + 9.2 + 9.1 + 9.3 + 9.4 = 55.2; 55.2 ÷ 6 scores = 9.2)

Page 25 Martin's batting average was .609. (14 hits ÷ 23 times at bat = .609)
His batting average was 26 percent higher than Cabrera's. (.609 = 61 percent; 61 percent − 35 percent = 26 percent)

Do the Math!
You strike out two to three batters for every six innings you pitch. (8 strikeouts ÷ 20 innings pitched = 0.4; 0.4 × 6 innings = 2.4 batters, or between 2 and 3 batters)

Page 27 Leah will end up at lacrosse camp. (Helen: 13 goals ÷ 8 games = 1.63 scoring average; 9 saves ÷ [9 saves + 3 goals] = 0.75 save percentage; 1.63 scoring average + 0.75 save percentage = 2.38); (Leah: 15 goals ÷ 8 games = 1.88 scoring average; 7 saves ÷ [7 saves + 4 goals] = 0.64 save percentage; 1.88 scoring average + 0.64 save percentage = 2.52); (Claire: 14 goals ÷ 8 games = 1.75 scoring average; 8 saves ÷ [8 saves + 4 goals] = 0.67 save percentage; 1.75 scoring average + 0.67 save percentage = 2.42)

Do the Math!
About 67 percent of the kids trying out will make the cut. (1 athlete + 35 athletes = 36 athletes; 12 spots per team × 2 teams = 24 spots; 24 spots ÷ 36 athletes = 0.67, or 67 percent)

Page 29 Ready, Set, Kick!
You will have to cover an extra 900 square yards (750 sq. m) on defense this season. (20 yds. × 30 yds. = 600 sq. yds.; 600 sq. yds. × 4 = 2,400 sq. yds.; 2,400 sq. yds. − 600 sq. yds. = 1,800 sq. yds.; 1,800 sq. yds. × ½ the field = 900 sq. yds.)
You will spend 20 extra minutes on the soccer field every Saturday. (4 quarters × 10 min. = 40 min.; 2 halves × 30 min. = 60 min.; 60 min. − 40 min. = 20 min.)
You will need to make between 21 and 37 more goals this year to match the coach's all-time best players. (16 games × 2 goals per game = 32 goals; 16 games × 3 goals per game = 48 goals; 32 goals − 11 goals = 21 goals; 48 goals − 11 goals = 37 goals)

Glossary

average: the sum of a group of numbers divided by the size of that group

compete: to try to win a game or contest against someone else

freestyle: a swimming event in which swimmers can use any stroke they choose

league: a group of sports teams that regularly play one another

meet: a sports competition, such as a track meet or a swim meet

play: an action or a move in a game

serve: to put a ball into play by hitting it over a net

set: one of three main periods of play in a tennis match

statistic: a number that represents a piece of information

Further Information

Cleary, Brian P. Illustrated by Brian Gable. *A Fraction's Goal: Parts of a Whole.* Minneapolis: Millbrook Press, 2011. Learn how fractions work with rhyming verse and a group of cats who divide everything they can find!

IXL Learning: Third Grade
http://www.ixl.com/math/grade-3
This site includes examples and practice problems to help you perfect your growing math skills.

Minden, Cecilia, and Katie Marsico. *Soccer.* Ann Arbor, MI: Cherry Lake Publishing, 2009. Check out this book for a closer look at how math shapes soccer!

PBS KIDS: Find It! Math and Sports
http://pbskids.org/cyberchase/find-it/math-and-sports
Visit this site for online games, videos, and activities that demonstrate the connection between math and sports.

Index